Pray Through the Middle

*A 31-Day Devotional Journal for Praying
Your Child Through Life Challenges*

Sonja W. Bachus

*Foreword by
Rev. Dr. C.L. Bachus, Pastor,
Mount Zion Baptist Church, Kansas City, KS*

Acknowledgements

This devotional journal is dedicated first to my late mother, Dr. Wilma Norman Bachus. Her prayers carried me and the many others whose lives she touched, including parents of wayward children, through the middle. My mother's love and patience were unrivaled and I am so grateful for her guidance and love. *"Rev. Daddy"*, C.L. Bachus, thank you so very much for consistently making your expectations clear and for both correction and a measure of (sometimes reluctant) grace when those expectations were not met. I am so thankful to you and mama for demonstrating and leading me to develop my own true relationship with Jesus Christ. It is this relationship with my Lord and Savior, that sustained me through some incredibly difficult life challenges to include my own middle and the loss of my mother during an already trying time in my life. To my brothers, Dr. Reggie, Dr. Selwyn Q., and Jerome, I love you and thank you for constantly supporting me through the good, the bad AND the middle. To my sister Verneda, oh how I love you! You marvelously and miraculously mentored me out of the middle and became my very best friend in the process. I thank my sisters-in-love; Detra for pragmatic advice and powerful prayers and Marla who answers my text or call anytime day or night. To my sons Darrian Sr. and DeAris Flint: I love you both SO MUCH! Even as adults, you are just precious to me. You, as I admittedly did with mama and daddy, have caused me some sleepless nights and plenty of grey hairs! Yet, in helping you navigate your middle; I drew closer to the Lord and ultimately wrote these devotions. Remember, as Grandma Wilma often reminded all of us, "Only what you do for Christ will last." Little Darrian, thank you for being my constant shadow and constant sidekick. I urge you to learn from our missteps and make good choices, so you avoid the pitfalls of the middle. Special thanks to my great friend MK for reading and providing feedback on this brief work, Ms. Courtney Hoskins, who though much younger than me, pushed and prodded me and my niece Bria Robinson for your help in getting to the finish line. To God be the glory!

Foreword

When I was asked to write the foreword in this devotional. I was somewhat taken aback. The first question I posed to myself was what makes my baby girl Sonja W. Bachus think I would be comfortable placing my name on a devotional she had written.

While she always loved and respected God and her family, and worked hard, during the middle as she refers to in the following pages, she gave me many of the gray hairs on my head.

However, for the Christian woman and mother she has become, I am more than over-joyed to write this short foreword to her devotional.

Anyone who has experienced real life, and especially those who have raised children, will greatly benefit from taking time to read this thirty-one day spiritual production, as I did when reading it. It was so spiritually fascinating until I said out loud…" you go girl."

Not only am I honored to offer these words, but I am also confident Sonja's mother, my late wife, Dr. Wilma Norman Bachus, would have been equally as proud of this undertaking.

Rev. C.L. "Clem" Bachus

Introduction

Proverbs 22:6
Train up a child in the way he should go,
and when he is old he will not depart from it.

The Bible teaches us to raise our children to live by God's commandments, study His word, confess and repent of sin, ultimately accepting Jesus Christ as Savior who died to cleanse us from sin while providing the gift of salvation and to devote our every effort to living for Him. The scripture advises that if we train up a child appropriately, when they are old they will not depart from this teaching. Oh, but what can happen in the middle! I classify the middle as that time when some of us don't make the best life choices even though we know how we should live. I must confess that I lived my own "middle" as I grew into adulthood and I can pretty accurately say that my parents at times wanted to strangle me, disown me and/or send me somewhere far away to put us all out of our misery. Looking back, I realize that what I thought of at the time as asserting my independence was, in fact, rebellion against all I had been taught, against my parents and ultimately against God. In effect, however, I suffered greatly and caused great suffering in my quest for independence and to prove that even though I was a P.K. (preacher's kid), I was just human and no different than everyone else. In retrospect I am just grateful my parents nor God gave up on me. As I have experienced my own children's journeys and watched the children of friends and family going through their respective "middle" experiences, I have dealt with some of the same feelings my parents must have had of fear, extreme worry, anger and on some days, overwhelming despair. For this reason, I share this 31-day devotional guide to praying for your child who is in the middle. Even if you are not experiencing challenges or trials as your child grows into adulthood, you can focus 31 days in special prayer for your child. With God's help and the wise counsel of my own parents, my faith and obedience have grown exponentially, and I have learned to do exactly what my parents did for me; starting and ending with prayer mixed with plenty of reality checks and loving yet firm accountability conversations. It is my hope and prayer that your 31 days spent in focused, intercessory prayer will bring about the change in direction you desire to see in your child. I pray that you will take comfort in knowing that with God all things are possible.

Love and Blessings,
Sonja W. Bachus
Survivor of "The Middle"
#survivorofthemiddle #praythroughthemiddle #31dayspraying

❦ Day 1 / Date:

Joshua 24:15
And if it is evil in your eyes to serve the LORD, choose this day whom you will serve, whether the gods your fathers served in the region beyond the river, or the gods of the Amorites in whose land you dwell. But as for me and my house, we will serve the LORD."

I remember the day my father had the sign installed next to the front door of the home I grew up in. It was made of brown plexiglass with white letters in all caps:

AS FOR ME AND MY HOUSE
WE WILL SERVE THE LORD OUR GOD
-THE BACHUSES

I also remember that to live in our home was to serve the Lord. PERIOD. This declaration front and center on our home was a definite conversation starter with friends. At 1720 there were some non-negotiables. In our home we heard and learned the word. We attended and were active in church. We prayed and we were prayed for. We were to strive for excellence and carry ourselves in a way that honored both our family name and God. While that sign triggered plenty of questions from friends and others, sometimes ridicule or teasing, I believe it subconsciously became a source of pride and a clear reminder of that expectation to honor God in the way we lived. Equally as important, this scripture and remembrance of that visible declaration, became a foundational element of how we have attempted to raise our own children. If you have laid a strong biblical foundation in your home, it is probable your child will avoid making poor choices and/or hitting that phase I call the middle. Yet, we live in a fallen world with more external influences than ever, so it is possible at some point you will or have already seen them make decisions that send you to your knees.

Pray:
Ask God to give your children the desire and strength to live in service to Him and reveal His promises in their lives.

Deuteronomy 6: 6-7
These commandments that I give you today are to be on your hearts. Impress them on your children. Talk about them when you sit at home and when you walk along the road, when you lie down and when you get up.

When my sons were in junior high and high school many of their friends liked to come over to our house where mixed with love and good food was plenty of real advice and what I will call very clear instruction on what I expected of them and their friends in terms of behavior. They dubbed my strong and quite passionate instruction as fussing. While my sons sometimes cringed and their friends laughed, they all knew that what they heard from me came from a place of love and concern about them as they grew into young men. I found myself sounding very much like my parents as I admonished them to "Make good choices." Don't do everything the crowd does; set yourself apart as something special." "Give God your time and talents." "If you take care of the small things God will bless you with even bigger things to take care of." "Treat others well. Treat them like you'd want to be treated." "Respect the girls you date and don't do ANTYHING with or to them you wouldn't want done with or to your mother. "With God on your side you can do ANYTHING." Although my sons are now adults, I still share wise counsel with them daily. As parents, we are called to build a strong foundation on which our children are able to build their lives and faith. While the foundation may be shaken at times, when we have taught well, in the long run, the foundation will stand.

Pray:
Ask God to lead your child to listen, absorb and demonstrate the lessons and wisdom you share with them.

❧ Day 3 / Date:

1 John 5:18
Because Jesus keeps them safe, the wicked one does not touch them.

Satan is always on the attack. As a matter of fact, he works harder at his job for more hours in a day than any of us could ever imagine working at ours; and many of us work pretty hard. The joy in all this is we can take comfort in knowing that Jesus, born of God, has the power and ability to keep them safe from all harm. Does this mean there will be no hard times and no trials will come the way of our children? It does not. What it does mean, though, is quite the opposite. It means that Satan can use all of his best ploys and send his best soldiers, but our Savior can keep them safe and not allow him to touch them. It says if we believe God's promises, we truly do not have to worry about them because Jesus is a "fence all around them" every day. A typical parent's nature and even more, a mother's nature is to worry; particularly about her children and ESPECIALLY if a child is going through the middle. As parents and believers, we must stand strong in the knowledge that God is a mighty protector and they are ultimately safe and secured by the covering of Jesus Christ himself.

Pray:

Pray for the strength to stand firm in God's word and remove worry from your mind.
Ask God to continue to keep them safe from harm and the ploys of the devil.
Thank God in advance for keeping them safe through the middle.

❧ Day 4 / Date:

1 John 5:21
Little children, guard yourselves from idols.

This passage of scripture reminds us not to place anything or anyone before God, transforming those things into idols. Idols might be sports, friends, jobs, drugs, clothes and shoes, money, cars and/or relationships, not necessarily in that order. Many of our children, especially when they are in the middle seem to forget that none of these things will bring them real peace and none of these things will grant them salvation. It is not enough to teach this concept. We must first be careful what we model for them. How we spend our time and where we place our priorities has a major effect on where our children will place theirs. It is also vitally important to remain faithful to continually reminding them to give God their time. My mother used to frequently remind us that if we could go to school and/or work forty or more hours per week, find time to hang out with friends and all the other activities we could find time for, we could surely give God at the very least a few hours on Sunday for Sunday School and worship. As young people go through the stages of feeling as if they are invincible and believing they have plenty of time and life ahead of them, they tend to place so many other priorities before God. Let's pray for them to set and stick to the right priorities; not allowing any of them become idols they place before God.

Pray:
   Pray for your child to set priorities and place God first.
   Pray for wisdom and patience in giving them guidance with respect to priorities.
   Ask God to guide you in modeling how to set priorities according to HIS will.

Isaiah 54:17
No weapon that is formed against thee shall prosper; and every tongue that shall rise against thee in judgement thou shalt condemn. This is the heritage of the servants of the Lord and their righteousness is of me saith the Lord.

Being obedient to God's will and striving to live a Godly life does not guarantee an easy life with no enemies or life trials. We know that the devil will use all manner of evil to attempt to destroy us. God did not promise us that weapons wouldn't be formed against us, however, He has promised that those weapons wouldn't prosper. In other words, He won't allow them to be successful in the attempts to bring us down. In the 54th chapter of Isaiah we are assured of this specifically. God tells us clearly that just by virtue of being His children we are gifted this legacy and promise.

It may be difficult when we are watching a child go through the middle to fully rely on this promise. Still, no matter how difficult, frustrating, or powerless we feel in the moment, we must find the strength to trust this promise and know that He can and will bring us AND our child through with Him having the victory over the enemy.

Pray:
Pray for God to tangibly reveal this promise in your life and the life of your child. Be intentional. List the "weapon(s)" you see being used against you/your child and locate a scriptural promise to pray against each one.

James 1: 2-4

Consider it pure joy my brothers and sisters when you face trials of many kinds, because you know that the testing of your faith produces perseverance. Let perseverance finish its work so that you may be mature and complete, not lacking anything.

How in the world could <u>anyone</u>, including God, think there should be joy in facing trials? Leave it to God to tell the writer of James to take us in the exact opposite direction we would most want to go to reveal Himself in our lives. Personally, I would prefer to get straight to the unwavering faith status without the trials. Knowing this is the obvious choice, I am also keenly aware that our heavenly father in His infinite wisdom allows us to weather storms in life to ultimately reveal His power, His goodness and most of all, His love. When our faith is tested, we are often tempted to give up. What we must ultimately give up is trying to "fix" things, wholly place our trust in God and persevere no matter the test; doing exactly what the word is instructing us to do in this passage. Know that if we refuse to endure and totally give up on God, we miss out on getting to that place of growth and maturity the Father has for us. That place where we can see the sun in a situation before it rises, where we can see the silver in the storm cloud's lining before the rain ceases and where we can see our child on the other side of the middle long before they get there.

Pray:

Ask God to increase your faith and allow you to persevere and grow in spiritual maturity while helping you to deal with any pressures you are currently facing.

✍ Day 7 / Date:

Philippians 4: 12-13
I know how to be abased, and I know how to abound. Everywhere and in all things, I have learned both to be full and to be hungry, both to abound and to suffer need. I can do all things through Christ who strengthens me.

When Paul wrote these lines, he had been through more than enough. Still, he found contentment in His relationship with Christ. He asserted that he could be rich or poor, well fed or starving, free or imprisoned, have plenty or have nothing but still he could stand tall and say, "I can do all things through Christ who strengthens me". While I have learned to be content in the midst of many difficult circumstances throughout my life, I still struggle miserably when it comes to my babies. As parents we want to see those young people who are still and will always be our babies have the best possible life; as good, or even better, than we had. We want them to listen, learn and skip making the mistakes we and others made. We still want to fix all their problems, heal their hearts and minds, and ensure they have a smooth life. If we could control all, no real problems would cross their paths and the middle would be a short blip and distant memory. As a matter of fact, there wouldn't be a "middle" at all if the decision were ours. What can we learn from this scripture passage? We can learn that no matter the situation, God is in control. We must learn to settle down and ride out the stormy as well as the sunny days and that we can do anything through the strength placed in us through Christ Jesus including praying a child through the middle.

Pray:
Ask God for the strength to accept tough circumstances with as much grace and thanksgiving as when they are good.

✥ Day 8 / Date:

Psalms 34:1
I will bless the Lord at all times; His praises shall continually be in my mouth. My soul shall make its boast in the Lord. The humble shall hear of it and be glad. Oh, magnify the Lord with me; And let us exalt his name together.

A few years ago, I quit making New Year's Resolutions and began reaffirming this scripture at the beginning of the year. I came to the conclusion that if I was living by this scripture, I could accomplish all the things us humans vow to do better in the new year. For, if I am blessing the Lord at all times, I will eat right, exercise to keep my physical temple healthy, treat others right, guard my thoughts and words, and give my best in everything I do. I continuously work on getting better at this every day. Why is my new year affirmation relevant to praying a child through the middle? As you well know, it's awfully easy to bless God in all things when life is going well. Home...check. Church...check. Job...check. Car...check. Bills paid on time... check. Kids doing well...check. Let any one of those elements unravel and our reactions might very quickly change. You may not be guilty of this, but I tell you when my sons both hit that place in the middle; things got real shaky and some days they still are. Yet, I've also learned that we must first keep praying and then praising, blessing, and ultimately trusting God; even when we feel completely crushed by life's circumstances. Remember when your prayers and praises go up; blessings come down.

Pray:

Ask God for the ability to continue to praise and bless Him at all times despite the circumstances with our child. Practice actively praising God in advance; first just for who He is and second, for what you know He can and will do.

❧ Day 9 / Date:

Philippians 4: 6-7
Be anxious for nothing, but in everything by prayer and supplication, with thanksgiving, let your requests be made known to God, and the peace of God which surpasses all understanding, will guard your hearts and minds through Christ Jesus.

Do you get anxious, worried, and stressed out about your children? I definitely do! I thought I was the strongest person alive because I had been through so much as a single parent raising two sons and "made it", Yet the reality of worrying and fretting over a child; not sleeping, not eating or eating too much, exhaustion, fatigue, anxiety, depression. Any or all these physical and emotional issues can come with being anxious and worried about a child. But they accomplish nothing more than killing joy when deep down we know that the only real answer is prayer and trusting God. Isaiah 26: 3-4 is another reminder of God's power to give us peace if we trust in him. "Those of steadfast mind you keep in peace—because they trust in you. Trust in the Lord forever, for in the Lord God you have an everlasting rock. Know that if we pray and then listen to what God says back to us, He alone can calm our fears.

Pray:
Ask God to calm your fears, help you not to worry and bring you peace. Practice deep breathing when you feel anxious. If possible, get to a quiet place to talk to God when the anxiety hits. If you can't get to a quiet place, pray right where you are.

Psalm 34: 8
Oh, taste and see that the Lord is good; Blessed is the man who trusts in Him!

God really is good! He is omniscient, omnipresent and always on time. Trust Him and He will deliver. He will show you over and over again that He really is good! Because we are human and fallible, we will sometimes fall into moments and/or seasons of doubt. Even as believers, we need to be reminded from time to time, and especially when we are facing storms, that God is still good, and we can trust Him at His word. There will inevitably be times when situations don't move according to our timing or turn out as we desire, yet we are compelled to keep trusting Him. Psalm 27:13 says, "I would have lost heart, unless I had believed that I would see the goodness of the Lord in the land of the living". I can't say it's easy. As a matter of fact, remembering that He is good and still in the blessing business is probably the most difficult task we have to accomplish each day when life gets hard. The key is in trusting His timing, knowing that we will see His goodness and there will be a testimony coming out of these trials.

Pray:
Ask God for the clarity to consistently see and acknowledge that He is always good. Pray that God will also show your child how good He is. Challenge yourself to identify at least one way God is good in your life and the life of your child each day.

❧ Day 11 / Date:

Ephesians 6:12
For we do not wrestle against flesh and blood, but against principalities, against powers, against rulers of the darkness of this age, against spiritual hosts of wickedness in the heavenly places.

When we are dealing with trials, we immediately look at the actual circumstance of the moment. Those immediate circumstances such as physical or mental health issues, disobedience, wayward living, alcohol and/or drug abuse and more cause us headache and heartache. But, if we step back and examine these circumstances, they aren't just random happenstance. They are well planned, carefully thought-out attacks waged by the enemy whose sole job is to try to break us. The real war is not with the circumstance. The circumstance is the vehicle used by the enemy to wage war on us. The true battle is with Satan and his team of "rulers of darkness" and "spiritual hosts of wickedness", and he will use every weapon in his arsenal including making weapons of our children if he can. Furthermore, the closer we get to God; the better we will fare in these battles. In contrast, the more we pray and then demonstrate our faith and trust in Him, the greater these forces war against us. I have experienced firsthand, times in my own journey, when the closer I grew to God, the more I prayed, attended church, gave to support ministry, displayed kindness, and progressed in my career and other areas in my life, the greater attack the enemy waged including striking against or through my children.

Pray:
Identify the evil forces you and your children are battling against and pray for victory over them.

❧ Day 12 / Date:

Psalms 130:5
I wait for the Lord, my soul waits, And in His word I do hope.

If you are anything at all like me and most people I know, you do not like to wait. Waiting is hard! It takes patience which some of us don't have much of. I have literally been praying and waiting on God for more than seven years to answer one specific prayer. There are times when I wait patiently. There are other times I am asking God why He won't hurry up and answer my prayer and then there are times I get angry and weary and can barely even talk to God because in my waiting I get to the place where I just have nothing left. One of my good friends shared with me that when she went through a really tough time with her family, she was so exhausted with all the waiting and trying to remain hopeful one particular night her prayer was simply "Look here God. You know what I'm going through, and you know what I need. Now I'm going to bed. Amen." It's just "like that" sometimes. This quote from lifequotes101.online says "Patience is not an ability to wait, but the ability to keep a good attitude while waiting." Fortunately, God really does know just what we need and all that He has promised in His word will be fulfilled. Hold on to hope. His answer and his provision are on the way.

Pray:

Ask God to give you the ability to wait for His answer and the ability to keep a good attitude while waiting.

Remember that your child, in spite of their own actions, is watching you and needs to be encouraged by seeing your trust in God.

❧ Day 13 / Date:

Ephesians 4:32
And be kind to one another, tenderhearted, forgiving one another, even as God in Christ forgave you.

Do you tend to get really angry with your children when they make what you may consider dumb choices and then more times than not, expect you to "fix" things for them? There are times when choices are made with no real consideration of the potential consequences. In my own case, I pray for the strength to forgive them for causing unnecessary heartache in spite of all I have done for them even into adulthood. As much as we love our children, there are likely times it is very difficult to forgive and even harder to forget. Working on being obedient to Ephesians 4:32 for me is a daily task. I often think about how a difficult conversation might turn out if I am kind and tenderhearted instead of angry and belligerent. Would displaying just a little grace turn the tide? Might they take another step in the right direction if a little more patience is offered? What happens when we immediately forgive them for the bad choices and transgressions instead of shouting and escalating the situation? As for me, I am definitely a work in progress. I am so thankful for a forgiving God who loved us so much He was willing to give up His Son for each one of us. The least we can do is forgive and be kind even when it is hard to do. How do you respond to your child's mistakes and missteps?

Pray:
Reflect on your reactions to your child's behaviors and choices. Pray that God will lead you to be kind, tenderhearted and forgiving with your child.

❧ Day 14 / Date:

Colossians 3:20
Children, obey your parents in all things, for this is well pleasing to the Lord.

I LOVE this scripture. It gives me the chance to be "right" and remind my sons who the boss is, and that not only does it make me happy, but God is pleased when they obey. I get the opportunity to tell them they best get to obeying God's command in this passage; hoping and praying they will follow my direction and not make any more mistakes or make me "look bad" as a parent based on their actions. Have you ever heard the saying: "If at first you don't succeed, do it the way mom told you the first time."? A few years ago, my oldest son asked me how I knew how almost every situation would turn out. I had to admit to him that I only knew because I didn't always listen to my parents' wise counsel and made many mistakes that I had to learn from. So, like my parents I could see the pitfalls ahead because I had experienced them firsthand or knew someone who had. I must admit that I can get so busy reminding my sons they are to obey me as their parent, I forget they are to obey, not just because I want them to, but because it is first and foremost an active display of obedience to God.

Pray:
Pray that your child will heed your words and warnings.
Ask God to help them be obedient to His will.

✤ Day 15 / Date:

Nehemiah 4:14

And I looked, and arose and said to the nobles, to the leaders, and to the rest of the people, "Do not be afraid of them. Remember the Lord, great and awesome, and fight for your brethren, your sons, your daughter, your wives, and your houses."

Since becoming a mother, I have been more concerned about something bad happening to my children over and above something happening to me or anyone else in my life. So naturally, as a parent, when a child is in the middle, one of the first reactions is fear. We fear what people will say about them or about us as parents. We fear that something terrible will happen to them. Instead of being afraid, it is imperative that we abandon the fear and get ready to fight; not physically, as God will fight our battles, but fight with the word and with steadfast prayer. Psalm 27:1-3 says "The Lord is my light and my salvation—whom shall I fear? The Lord is the stronghold of my life—of whom shall I be afraid? When the wicked advance against me to devour me, it is my enemies and my foes who stumble and fall. Though armies besiege me, my heart will not fear; though war break out against me, even then I will be confident". The middle is the enemy, and we must not be afraid because we can believe and know based on His past performance, that God is greater than the enemy. He is stronger than any challenge. He is great. He is awesome God and ultimately, He is in control.

Pray:

Ask God to calm your fears and choose at minimum one concrete tactic such as reciting Nehemiah 4:14 or Psalm 27: 1-3 to help you calm your fears.

❧ Day 16 / Date:

Isaiah 49:14-16
But Zion said, "The Lord has forsaken me, and my Lord has forgotten me." "Can a woman forget her nursing child, and not have compassion on the son of her womb? Surely, they may forget, yet I will not forget you. See, I have inscribed you on the palms of my hands; Your walls are continually before Me."

Even when it feels like God has gone silent, never forget that He is always right there. When your child is in the middle and you are praying and, in my case, nonstop petitioning, for God to move you may THINK God is not paying attention. I remind you He is always right there. He has not forgotten you. Not only are we inscribed on the palms of His hands, in Psalm 139:13 we are reminded that He formed our inward parts and knitted us together in our mother's womb. For nearly three years I was convinced that God had forgotten me. Not only did it feel like He had forgotten me, but I was also even more convinced that He had forgotten my children and left them out in the world to be destroyed. I'd been praying for a breakthrough for one of my sons and on top of all he was going through it seemed that everything else in my life was slowly crumbling. The amazing thing about this period of time was I had this life that looked nearly picture perfect from the outside while inside I was barely hanging on. I most definitely knew the meaning of "My God, My God why has thou forsaken me?" One day, seemingly suddenly and out of the blue, everything started to move. While I was feeling lost and forgotten, God was moving in ways I could not have imagined. Keep in mind, He sometimes moves quietly with no fanfare. Remain confident in the fact that God is ALWAYS moving.

Pray:
Ask God to keep you, comfort you and speak clearly to you when it seems He has forgotten you. Spend time in meditation focusing on listening to God.

Isaiah 49:25
But thus says the Lord: "Even the captives of the mighty shall be taken away, and the prey of the terrible delivered; For I will contend with him who contends with you, and I will save your children."

God promised! He promised protection. He promised to contend with the enemy and to save our children. Personally, I take this promise quite literally. God had promised the children of Israel that He would deliver them although they had to go through the captivity as a result of their disobedience and idolatry. There are times that one must suffer the consequences of choices and actions. Those choices many times also affect others. Yet, the Lord promises that those who exact the punishment and terror unjustly won't win and there is deliverance from those circumstances. Relief comes in His time, in His way. When Satan mounts his massive attacks, he must also realize that his efforts will ultimately be defeated by the powerful forces of the almighty God. While we are in that captivity it is difficult to see but we must trust that God will keep His word and remove us from the hand of the enemy.

Pray:

Ask God to deliver your child. Make a list the ways in which God has delivered you or others before as a reminder to both you and God what He can and will do in times of trouble.

❧ Day 18 / Date:

Daniel 1: 11-15

So Daniel said to the steward whom the chief of the eunuchs had set over Daniel, Hananiah, Mishael and Azariah, "Please test your servants for ten days, and let them give us vegetables to eat and water to drink. Then let our appearance be examined before you, and the appearance of the young men who eat the portion of the king's delicacies; and as you see fit, so deal with your servants." So, he consented with them in this matter, and tested them for ten days. And at the end of ten days their features appeared better and fatter in flesh than all the young men who are the portion of the king's delicacies.

Is it time to fast and pray? YES! As we pray for our children and sacrifice (food, social media, spending, etc.) we have the ability to move our prayers to a higher plane through fasting. The Bible teaches us about fasting in both the old and new testaments. Nehemiah fasted and prayed for his people and ultimately rebuilt the wall around Jerusalem. Ezra fasted and prayed for protection. Jesus fasted; conquering temptation by Satan when His flesh was at its weakest. He displayed His unwavering faith in the Father and prepared Himself for the ultimate sacrifice. Paul and Barnabas fasted in worship before being sent out to spread the gospel. Choosing to add a period of fasting to your prayer life is a very personal spiritual decision. It is critical to consult the Father in prayer even as you contemplate a fast. While fasting is not a required element of prayer, fasting can move you to a new level of dependence on God for strength and perseverance.

Pray:
Ask God to guide your prayer and fasting for your child and to sustain you through your chosen fast.

Daniel 3: 16-18
Shadrach, Meshach, and Abed-Nego answered and said to the king, "O, Nebuchadnezzar, we have no need to answer you in this matter. If that is the case, our God whom we serve is able to deliver us from the burning fiery furnace, and He will deliver us from your land, O king. But, if not, let it be known to you, O king, that we do no serve your gods, nor will we worship the gold image which you have set up".

And if not, HE IS STILL GOD and HE is STILL GOOD.

God answers ALL prayers. He may not answer in the manner we desire; yet He answers them all. One of the most difficult realizations we must come to accept is that not getting the outcome we have prayed for gives us no right to decide God is not still good. Sincerely asking God to bring a child through the middle does not guarantee that His will is to bring them through quickly, to grant the desired or requested outcome, or frankly, to bring them through at all. The Hebrew boys demonstrated a strong committed faith in God's ability to keep them from death in the fiery furnace. Additionally, their acceptance of and declaration that even if God did not save them, they would not bow to Nebuchadnezzar, demonstrated for us that they had determined that even if not, HE IS STILL GOD and HE is STILL GOOD. When praying for your children, know that God can and will answer your prayers. At the same time, recognize that how God answers your prayers is according to His will. Even if He does not answer HOW you've asked, HE IS STILL GOD and HE is STILL GOOD.

Pray:
Ask God to help you accept His will regardless of the outcome.

Proverbs 3: 5-6
Trust in the Lord with all your heart and lean not unto your own understanding; In all your ways acknowledge Him, And He shall direct your paths.

This passage of scripture was one of my mother's favorites. As such, we learned from an early age through her teaching that we could not rely solely on ourselves, or even other humans since none of us have the Father's divine discernment. We were taught that we must fully rely on God for direction. When we are walking through times of difficulty in our lives with our children it is easy to fall into attempting to fix all the problems they are facing. As parents and humans in general, our first response after the natural shock, anger, fear and/or panic reactions, is almost always to try and fix everything we can for our children. What we must learn to do is remind ourselves that we are first to go to God; trusting Him to give us clarity and direction. We must learn to pause and to breathe, then pray and patiently listen for direction. We have direct access to His infinite wisdom. He knows so much more than we do and ultimately controls the outcome whether we try to fix it or not. Isaiah 55:8-9 says "For my thoughts are not your thoughts, neither are your ways my ways" declares the Lord. "As the heavens are higher than the earth, so are my ways higher than your ways and my thoughts than your thoughts. Trust God. Seek His will and allow Him to guide not only your steps but your reactions in times of trouble.

Pray:
   Ask God how to respond to trouble. Be still. Wait and listen for His all-knowing direction.

❧ Day 21 / Date:

1 John 2: 24-25

Therefore, let that abide in you which you heard from the beginning. If what you heard from the beginning abides in you, you also will abide in the Son and the Father. And this is the promise that He has promised us—eternal life.

Do not let this truth get away from you! You KNOW the truth. You KNOW the power of our almighty God. You KNOW that through Him and Him alone we are saved. As written in this scripture passage, we don't have to learn anything new as we face life's challenges and trials. The same truths and principles apply to anything we face, including circumstances with a child. Even when a child isn't demonstrating it, when we have exposed them to a strong foundation of biblical teaching and living, deep down in their heart and mind they know the only way to true joy is through Jesus Christ and their walk should show that understanding. When we watch our child traipsing haphazardly through the middle, circumstances may not reflect this knowledge, yet God's truths never change. It is these truths that become the "still small voice" in the back of their minds and the depths of their hearts; providing a compass until they come to themselves. It is also these truths that will keep us on course as we navigate the choppy waters of worry and fear. During tough times be sure to hold on to this truth and divine promise. Do not let them get away from you.

Pray:

Ask God to help you abide in His truth and boldly expect Him to keep His promises for the earthly and eternal life for you and your child.

1 John 5:14-15
This is the confidence which we have before Him, that, if we ask anything according to His will, He hears us. And if we know that He hears us, whatever we ask, we know that we have the petitions that we have asked of Him.

When we ask other human beings for help, consideration, favors, etc., even those we are closest to and know intimately, we don't really know what the response will be This unknown may cause hesitance or fear when considering making a request for support. In stark contrast to making requests of others, with God there is no fear. We can go boldly to the Father in prayer with our requests on behalf of our child with full confidence that He will answer according to His will for both their and our lives. HIS will. I admit that the caveat of HIS will can be painfully difficult to accept, yet we know and must accept that His will is perfect even in the difficult and stormy seasons of life. It is critical that we exercise confidence in going to God with full faith and expectation that He will answer our prayers for Him to move in our children's lives. Still, we must be careful in remembering that the answers are His to give and not ours to dictate. Personally, I am still working on this and daily asking God to advance me to fully seeking His will instead of expecting Him to move to mine.

Pray:
Ask God to align your prayers with His will and to move in the circumstances you face with your child.

1 Peter 5:6-7
Therefore humble yourselves under the mighty hand of God, that He may exalt you in due time, casting all your cares upon Him, because He cares for you.

Two key thoughts arise when I read this scripture. First, there is a call for humility. You are likely not guilty of this, however, I occasionally find myself displaying a bit of "righteous indignation". This happens when I start thinking of how hard I've worked to be a good mother, teaching my children about the love of Jesus and providing a good life as a good mother should. Next, I start asking God why He would allow pain and stress into my life after the things I'd gotten right; why He would allow the enemy to pursue MY children. As I am asking these questions, He immediately and consistently reminds me that what I believe has earned me a pass on troubles related to my child, is no guarantee of ease. He reminds me to remain humble and to recognize that the pain He has allowed into my life is ultimately for His glory. It doesn't feel good in the moment, yet the premise and promise of 1 Peter 5:6-7 is that He is there for us to cast our cares upon and He cares for us like no other. The comfort of His love and care for His children is greater than the pain any "middle" our child goes through may bring.

Pray:

Ask God to help you remain humble, understand that you can't "earn" away troubles from your life or the life of your child and to trust Him in spite of the circumstances.

Repeat this positive affirmation from the scripture passage as often as you need to: "He cares for me."

❧ Day 24 / Date:

Romans 8:28
And we know that all things work together for the good to those who love God, to those who are the called according to His purpose.

This proclamation is certainly easier read and said than done. When everything turns out right it is easy to confidently quote Romans 8:28. When fear, pain, worry, and stress combine to make life so hard it seems unbearable, we may even quote this scripture through the pain and heartache. Still, there are times when it is downright difficult to see circumstances we consider bad as working for the good, even for those of us called according to His purpose. Yet, how we respond is critical. Paul talked of his thorn in the flesh and of being made strong through weakness. He even directed us in James 1:2 "Count it all joy when we fall into diverse trials." WHAT??? The truth of the matter is that how we respond does have the power to define personal outcomes. When we allow the Father's truths to permeate our thinking and responses, our mental and physical health can withstand the trials we are facing. When we allow the realities we see in front of us to overshadow His truths and our faith, we lose sleep, eat too much or too little, make poor choices and damage our physical and emotional health. This is my admission that my responses aren't always great; at least at the outset; especially where my children are concerned. Yet, in the long run, I must return to the realization that for those who love Him and are called according to His purpose, He will weave all things together for good.

Pray:
Ask God for faith to trust that all things will work together for good in the life of your children. Ask Him to direct your response when you face these hard times in life.

❧ Day 25 / Date:

Luke 22:31-32
And the Lord said, "Simon, Simon! Indeed, Satan has asked for you, that he may sift you as wheat. But I have prayed for you, that your faith should not fail; and when you have returned to Me, strengthen your brethren."

When there is great potential, the attack is even greater. Satan is greedy and he is bold; bold and audacious enough to go right to God to ask for access to His children. While God is our protector, He sometimes allows the enemy to attack. As painful as life can be we must know that it is ultimately for the greater good. From great tests come greater testimonies. This example in the book of Luke follows another well-known example in the Old Testament where Satan asked for Job and then wreaked all manner of havoc on Job's life; so much so that Job's own wife told him to just curse God and die. Still, these two, two of God's very best, remained faithful, put their trust in God and came away able to encourage others and now us with their testimony. As we walk through difficult times, we are being put to that test that will yield the testimony and glorify God. In the midst of a trial, it may not feel that way. As difficult as it is to do, we must also move out of the way so God can work in the life of our child. God is depending on us to bring hope to others as we pray with and for our children and preparing us to give encouragement and hope to others experiencing similar pain.

Pray:
Ask God to give you the strong faith to endure the test and the courage to share the resulting testimony.

Jeremiah 29: 11-13

For I know the thoughts that I think toward you, says the Lord, thoughts of peace and not of evil, to give you a future and a hope. Then you will call upon Me and go and pray to Me, and I will listen to you. And you will seek me and find Me, when you search for Me with all your heart.

God has a plan for us. God has a plan for our children. Like the Israelites, we go through some periods of trouble that seem as if they will last forever. This scripture is a message of amazing hope, yet we must also realize that it does not promise us He will end the suffering quickly. God intends for us to learn to truly depend on Him, to keep seeking Him and as such find peace in the midst of trouble. In my personal experience, I have found that God never gives me just one thing. During one not so distant period of my life, I faced so many major challenges, I could not see my way ever clearing any of them. Some of these challenges remain in my life, however, God has shown me more clearly than ever that God is truly a keeper. He has a unique way of proving to us that we can lean only on Him while giving us some contentment in our wilderness. You must know that God does have a plan for your life, and He has a plan for your child. Even when a child is in the middle He is right there with and for them and for us if we will only draw close to Him with all of our energy.

Pray:
Ask God to show you His thoughts toward you as you seek Him with all your heart.

Ephesians 4:29

"Let no corrupting talk come out of your mouths, but only such as is good for building up, as fits the occasion, that it may give grace to those who hear.

Have you heard the saying: "You get more flies than honey than you do with vinegar"? This simple idea puts Ephesians 4:29 into plain English. When we have a child who has made a bad decision or even completely gone astray, it is easy to lose our cool and respond in ways that actually make situations worse. Instead of creating an environment that causes them to listen, reflect and build confidence in working through the situation, the focus turns to the delivery and feelings it triggered. I wish I could say my responses are consistently loving and supportive while being firm and encouraging improvement and accountability. Proverbs 15:1 says, "A soft word turns away wrath, but a harsh word stirs up anger." This is where the popular concept of mindfulness intersects perfectly with our spiritual lives. Pause. Take a deep breath, absorbing the immediate reaction and exhaling it. Focusing your breath, mind, and heart on responding with grace and loving correction and/or direction can completely turn a situation around. Know with certainty that responding with love does not equal the absence of appropriate boundaries or compromising foundationally. In fact, this is how God has directed us to respond.

Pray:

Ask God to give you the calm and clarity to speak with love and grace when angry or disappointed with your child.

❧ Day 28 / Date:

Luke 15:23-24
And bring the fatted calf here and kill it, and let us eat and be merry; for this my son was dead and is alive again; he was lost and is found. And they began to be merry.

The story of the prodigal son who asked for and squandered his inheritance while his father was still living is a familiar one. Just as the father in the biblical parable likely prayed for the day his son would come to his senses, we pray for and look forward to that day when our children get to the other side of their middle. I remember my mother speaking of praying for eight years or more for God to change a situation. I dare say that those prayers were for me. I also remember that no matter how many bad decisions I made or how disappointed she was, she consistently showed me love. It was that love and her prayers that helped me move through my own personal middle. When your child is in the middle remember to also show them love, grace and forgiveness. You may have to forgive them over and over just as God does with us. With God's help prayerfully the day will come for that celebration when the situation changes for the better.

Pray:
Ask God to allow you to eagerly forgive your child and show them the love they need. Always be ready to welcome them with open arms so they are unafraid to return when they come to their senses as the prodigal son did.

❧ Day 29 / Date:

II Timothy 2:15
Study to show thyself approved unto God, a worker who does not need to be ashamed, rightly dividing the word of truth.

Life can be a battle. How can we battle back in hard times? Those in the military study, prepare and train for their daily operations and for the probability of war. They stay at the ready. Like the military studying their manuals and preparing we can only be prepared for life's battles if we are battlefield prepared. This we accomplish by being grounded in God's word. Our manual is our Holy Bible. Not only are we to read the Bible, but we must also pray for discernment and understanding. Spending time in the word gives us knowledge. It gives us direction. It teaches us how to respond. The Bible defines God's love for us and how that love is the foundation for healing and hope when we face difficult times. It is critical we know the word both to ground us during difficult times and prepare us to share the word and its wisdom with others, starting with our children.

Pray:
Set aside time to ready and study the word of God. Ask Him for insight and understanding as you find answers to the problems you face through gaining spiritual knowledge.

1 Peter 4:8
And above all things have fervent love for one another, for "love will cover a multitude of sins."

John 3:16-17
For God so loved the world that He gave His only begotten Son, that whoever believes in Him should not perish but have everlasting life. For God did not send His Son into the world to condemn the world, but that the world though Him might be saved.

John 15:12
This is my commandment, that you love one another as I have loved you. Greater love has no one than this, than to lay down one's life for his friends.

It all comes down to love. Love is the most powerful concept known to man. Everything in life truly comes down to love. God's love kept Him from striking Adam and Eve down for their disobedience in the garden. His love restored his servant Job. His love forgave David and allowed him to write some of the most beautiful words in the Bible. His love saved Daniel in the Lion's Den and the Hebrew boys in the fiery furnace. It was His ultimate and sacrificial love that sent his son to earth to die for us and be resurrected so that we could live in fellowship with Him on earth and then in eternity with Him in heaven. When we teach our children, discipline our children, fight for our children, hurt for our children, pray for our children, it is all because we love them. Yet, as much as we love them, God loves them far more and more completely than we ever could. We must learn to balance our love with knowing that because God loves them most, He can protect them better than we can, and He will also chastise them for their greater good. To love our children is to fully entrust them to God and His will for their lives.

Pray:
Ask God to let His love flow through you to your child in a manner that changes them for the better; pushing them through the middle to the other side where they are living as God would have them to.

❧ Day 31 / Date:

Mark 10:27
But Jesus looked at them and said, "With men it is impossible, but not with God; for with God all things are possible."

Are there are days when you wonder if there will ever be an end to the middle? When you have done all you can and you have talked until there are no more words, when you are weary and worn down, you must give the reins to the Father. When you have planned, prayed and pleaded in the attempt to get the "middle" out of the way and it still has persisted, you must stand down. The roller coaster of good and bad days, the fear and worry, the pleading with God to clear a path to success and stability seem never ending. What we must know and fully accept is that what we cannot do as mere mortals, even as loving parents, is fully possible with God.

I challenge you to get out of the way. No more attempting to manipulate His will. No more fixing every mistake. We may not be able to change the circumstances, yet we know there is one who can and will. I challenge you to lay down the heavy burden of thinking you can fix it on your own. I challenge you to declare with courage and confidence that with God ALL things are truly possible.

Prayer:

Father God, thank you for my child_____. Thank you for your son Jesus and His sacrifice for our salvation on the cross. We ask that you give us strength to turn those we love who need to align their actions with your will toward you and away from the world. We ask that as we grow closet to you through your word and worship, we will gain wisdom, power and hope as we submit them to you in prayer. We give them to you with full confidence that you can and will work miracles in their lives and move them out of the middle.

In Jesus holy and righteous name. Amen.

About the Author
Sonja W. Bachus

Sonja W. Bachus is the youngest of the five children of Rev. Dr. C.L. Bachus, Pastor of the Mount Zion Baptist Church of Kansas City, Kansas, and the late Dr. Wilma Norman Bachus. She was born in Helena, Arkansas and raised in Kansas City, Kansas. A preacher's kid "P.K.", Sonja was raised in a Christian home and was actively involved in her church as well as local, district and state activities.

Sonja is the mother of two adult sons and grandmother of four amazing grandchildren. As shared in the foreword of this devotional, Sonja knows a lot about the "middle" through which she found her way and from praying her own sons through some of the challenges they faced as they grew into young adults.

Sonja has worked in the healthcare industry for more than twenty years and is blessed to demonstrate her life's calling through her leadership in healthcare organizations serving in medically underserved communities.

Sonja holds a Bachelor of Business Administration from Washburn University, Topeka, KS and a Master of Jurisprudence in Health Law from Loyola University Chicago.